DRIVEN

A PHOTOBIOGRAPHY OF HENRY FORD

DRIVEN

A PHOTOBIOGRAPHY OF HENRY FORD

BY DON MITCHELL

FOREWORD BY LEE IACOCCA
Former President, Ford Motor Company

NATIONAL GEOGRAPHIC
WASHINGTON, D.C.

For my parents, Ken and Margaret Mitchell, who taught me the importance of history and the written word—and made everything possible

For information about special discounts for bulk purchases, please contact National Geographic Books Special Sales: ngspecsales@ngs.org

For rights or permissions inquiries, please contact National Geographic Books Subsidiary Rights: ngbookrights@ngs.org

PUBLISHED BY THE NATIONAL GEOGRAPHIC SOCIETY

John M. Fahey, Jr., *President and Chief Executive Officer*

Gilbert M. Grosvenor, *Chairman of the Board*

Tim T. Kelly, *President, Global Media Group*

John Q. Griffin, *Executive Vice President; President, Publishing*

Nina D. Hoffman, *Executive Vice President; President, Book Publishing Group*

Melina Gerosa Bellows, *Executive Vice President, Children's Publishing*

PREPARED BY THE BOOK DIVISION

Nancy Laties Feresten, *Vice President, Editor in Chief, Children's Books*

Jonathan Halling, *Design Director, Children's Publishing*

Jennifer Emmett, *Executive Editor, Reference and Solo, Children's Books*

Carl Mehler, *Director of Maps*

R. Gary Colbert, *Production Director*

Jennifer A. Thornton, *Managing Editor*

STAFF FOR THIS BOOK

Suzanne Patrick Fonda, *Editor*

Bea Jackson, *Art Director*

Lori Renda, *Illustrations Editor*

Marty Ittner, *Designer*

Priyanka Lamichhane, *Associate Editor*

Kathryn Murphy, *Editorial Intern*

Martin S. Walz, *Map Research and Production*

Anne Cherry, *Copy Editor*

Connie D. Binder, *Indexer*

Grace Hill, *Associate Managing Editor*

Lewis R. Bassford, *Production Manager*

Susan Borke, *Legal and Business Affairs*

MANUFACTURING AND QUALITY MANAGEMENT

Christopher A. Liedel, *Chief Financial Officer*

Phillip L. Schlosser, *Vice President*

Chris Brown, *Technical Director*

Nicole Elliott, *Manager*

Rachel Faulise, *Manager*

ACKNOWLEDGMENTS

I wish to thank Lee Iacocca for writing the Foreword to this book, and his assistant, Norma Saken, for her support. I'd also like to thank Norman Brauer for his insights into "the Vagabonds." Thanks also to the Benson Ford Research Center of the Henry Ford in Dearborn, Michigan, especially the following Research Center staff for their invaluable assistance in reviewing this manuscript and in helping to acquire and provide background information related to the images: Judith E. Endelman, director of the Benson Ford Research Center, Stephanie Lucas, Jim Orr, Linda Skolarus, and Kathy Steiner as well as curators Jeanine Head Miller and Bob Casey.

I am grateful to the staff of Children's Books, in particular, Nancy Laties Feresten, Jennifer Emmett, Marty Ittner, Lori Renda, Carl Mehler, and Martin Walz. I would like to offer special thanks to my editor, Suzanne Patrick Fonda, a consummate professional who has embodied the best of the National Geographic Society in over 30 years of dedicated service to that organization. Her contributions to this book are a fitting tribute to the memory of her father, Henry John Nave (1913–1993), who was inducted into the Automotive Hall of Fame in Dearborn, Michigan, for his accomplishments in the motor vehicle industry.

I have been fortunate to have the world's best parents, and this book is dedicated to them. Their love and support made everything possible for me. My father spent his career working with distinction and integrity in the automotive industry, and he sacrificed much to make sure that I had every opportunity. And as always, I am deeply grateful to my wife, Grace ("the Believer"), and my children, Logan and Ella—crickets on my hearth.

LIBRARY OF CONGRESS CATALOGING-IN-PUBLICATION INFORMATION

Mitchell, Don, 1957–

Driven : a photobiography of Henry Ford / by Don Mitchell.

p. cm.

Includes bibliographical references and index.

ISBN 978-1-4263-0155-1 (trade hardcover : alk. paper) —

ISBN 978-1-4263-0156-8 (library binding : alk. paper)

1. Ford, Henry, 1863–1947—Juvenile literature. 2. Automobile industry and trade—United States—Biography—Juvenile literature. 3. Industrialists—United States—Biography—Juvenile literature. I. Title.

TL140.F6M59 2010

338.7'6292092—dc22

[B] 2009007136

Printed in China

10/RRDS/1

PHOTO CREDITS: All images from the Collection of The Henry Ford except p. 5, Bettmann/Corbis; p. 6, public domain; p. 7, Ford Motor Company; p. 9 background, Miles Luzanin/Shutterstock; p. 51, *New York Times*/ Redux Pictures; p. 54 up Bettmann/ Corbis; p. 57, Bettmann/ Corbis; p. 60 left, Underwood & Underwood/ Corbis; p. 60 right, Hulton Archive/Getty Images; p. 61, Swim Ink 2, LLC/Corbis.

COVER: Henry Ford's first official portrait for Ford Motor Company, taken in 1904, is surrounded by images of the automaker's empire: a Model A assembly line *(left)*, the Highland Park machine shop *(top)*, and smokestacks of the vast River Rouge plant.

CASE COVER (TRADE EDITION): Images of early Ford vehicles

HALF TITLE PAGE: Charles Sheeler's 1927 photograph of crisscrossed conveyors and smokestacks captures the industrial might of Ford Motor Company's River Rouge plant.

FULL TITLE PAGE: Henry stands next to a 1921 Model T in Buffalo, New York.

OPPOSITE: Henry Ford drives the 1896 quadricycle, his first car, on a New York City street in 1910.

"I will build a motor car for the great multitude....large enough for the family but small enough for the individual....But it will be so low in price that no man making a good salary will be unable to own one — and enjoy with his family the blessing of hours of pleasure in God's great open spaces."

FOREWORD

A Ford advertisement from the 1920s

Henry Ford's Model T was hailed as America's Everyman Car when it rolled out in 1908. It was affordable, durable, and could go just about anywhere. Sunday drives in the country were no longer just for the rich. As this 1920s advertisement claims, Ford made the world a playground for everyone.

Growing up, my dream was to work for Ford Motor Company. My father, an immigrant worker from Italy, owned one of the first Model T's in Allentown, Pennsylvania, and my first car was a beat-up, 60-horsepower, 1938 Ford. In 1946 my dream came true.

Fresh out of college, I landed a job working as a trainee in a drafting room at the enormous River Rouge plant near Detroit. I was working on a mechanical drawing of a clutch spring when I heard a big commotion. There, at one end of the floor, stood Henry Ford with aviation pioneer Charles Lindbergh. They started walking up and down the aisles, talking to the workers. I was awestruck. I just hoped they wouldn't ask me a question. I had been there only 30 days, and I didn't have a clue what I was doing.

The boss was a genius, and his mark on history is extraordinary. Ford was from modest, agrarian Michigan roots. He thought that the guys who made cars

Lee Iacocca, leader of the design team for the Ford Mustang, poses with models of the car that helped make him president of Ford Motor Company in 1970—a position he held until 1978, when he went to work for Chrysler.

ought to be able to afford one themselves. He figured that if he paid his factory workers a real living wage and produced more cars in less time for less money, everyone would buy them. And they did.

Ford was smart enough to know that making a car wasn't enough. Just like horses, cars need to be fed, so he pushed for gas stations to be built everywhere. He established a dealer-franchise system to sell and service cars, and his campaign for better roads led to an interstate highway system that is still the envy of the world.

Henry Ford's crusade to create a mass market for cars put America's industrial revolution into overdrive and created a middle class. In *Driven,* Don Mitchell explores the life of this fascinating and complex man, who was the father of 20th-century American industry.

Lee Iacocca

Lee Iacocca, former president, Ford Motor Company

DON'T LET HENRY SEE THEM! HE'LL TAKE THEM APART!" Young Henry Ford's brothers and sisters had to guard their new windup toys to keep their oldest brother from getting his hands on them. Henry was always curious about how anything mechanical operated. But unlike most children who could take things apart, he usually could put them together again. He graduated from tinkering with simple children's toys to being able to repair pocket watches by the time he was 13. Henry became obsessed with studying and repairing timepieces, with their intricate, finely tuned mechanisms. As a neighbor said, "Every clock in the Ford home shuddered when it saw him coming."

Henry Ford was born into a world without electricity, in the upstairs bedroom of his parents' farmhouse. The family lived approximately ten miles west of Detroit, Michigan, in a rural area that is now part of Dearborn. The oldest of William and Mary Ford's six surviving children — four boys and two girls — Henry was born on July 30, 1863, just weeks after the Civil War battle at Gettysburg, Pennsylvania. His father, an immigrant from Ireland, was a prosperous farmer. His mother was the most important person in Henry's young life. When she died in 1875 at the age of 37, shortly after losing a baby in childbirth, 12-year-old Henry was devastated. He would later say, "The house was like a watch without a mainspring."

"There was too much hard hand labor on our own and all other farms of the time. Even when very young I suspected that much might somehow be done in a better way. That is what took me into mechanics."

This is the earliest surviving photograph of Henry Ford, taken when he was two and a half years old. In the background are the types of gears and watch mechanisms that Henry loved to tinker with as a boy.

Henry's mother, Mary Litogot Ford, and his father, William, are shown with the farmhouse where Henry was born and grew up. The house has been restored and can now be visited at Greenfield Village in Dearborn, Michigan.

Growing up, Henry experienced his share of the drudgery of farmwork. He particularly disliked milking cows and tending chickens. But the boy mechanic also brought his skills to the farm, repairing wagons, resetting the handles of tools, hammering out hinges at the family forge, and even inventing a device that enabled the driver of a wagon to open and close a farm gate without leaving his seat. Henry became convinced that the right machinery could make farm life much easier.

On a hot, clear day in July, 1876 — shortly before his 13th birthday — Henry and his father were riding in one of their farm wagons toward Detroit when they encountered something Henry had never seen before. A steam engine was traveling along the road under its own power. He would vividly recall that the vehicle "was simply a portable engine and boiler mounted on wheels with a water tank and coal cart behind." Henry had seen many of these engines hauled around by horses, "but this one had a chain that made a connection between the engine and the rear wheels of the wagon-like frame on which the boiler was mounted." Henry was astounded.

As soon as the vehicle stopped to allow the Fords to pass by, Henry jumped to the ground and excitedly began asking the driver questions about the steam engine. The man, clearly proud of his machine, was happy to explain how it worked to such an eager listener. The incident changed Henry's life. From that day forward, he became obsessed with "making a machine that would travel the roads" under its own power. Henry Ford would not invent the automobile, but more than any other single individual he would make it affordable for people from all walks of life.

By the time he was 15, Henry was anxious to taste life away from the farm. Henry liked school, but he also believed that "[t]here is an immense amount to be learned simply by tinkering with things. It is not possible to learn from books how everything is made — and a real mechanic ought to know how nearly everything is made. Machines are to a mechanic what books are to a writer." He dropped out of school and set off to nearby Detroit, which in 1879 was just coming into its own as an industrial center. Henry found work in several different machine shops, which produced everything from valves and fire hydrants to streetcars and ships. He was eager to learn all he could from the experienced workers. Indeed, this is where his real education began. Henry had no way of knowing that one day he would play a major role in making Detroit the automobile capital of the world.

In 1882 Henry, now 19, came home to help with the harvest. When the job was done, his father tried to persuade him to stay and take over the farm, but Henry had no interest in that. Instead, he followed his passion and took a job servicing steam engines throughout southern Michigan and northern Ohio, using the farm as his home base. Henry replaced his childhood toy shop with "a first-class workshop," where he experimented with gas engines and did other machine work every chance he got. His planned few weeks at home turned into several years.

In 1885, at a New Year's dance, 21-year-old Henry met 18-year-old Clara Jane Bryant. Clara was not only beautiful, she was also smart and serious. And Clara found the intense, music-loving Henry to be unlike any of the other young men she knew. The two spent time together going to dances, ice-skating parties, and riding in Henry's new green sleigh. In the summer the couple enjoyed picnics and buggy rides. Henry called Clara "The Believer" because of her faith in his abilities and his ideas. They married three years after meeting.

By 1890 Henry was working on an internal combustion engine fueled by gasoline. This relatively small and light engine intrigued Henry. He along with others thought it would be ideal to power a vehicle. But the firing cycle for this engine required electricity, a form of energy he didn't fully understand.

To learn more about it, he and Clara moved to Detroit, where Henry got a job as an engineer with the Edison Electric Illuminating Company. This new company provided electricity to about one thousand Detroit homes and thousands of the city's streetlights. Henry believed that there was no better place to get the education he needed than at the company founded by Thomas Edison.

Henry loved his new job tending a massive steam generator. With promotions came more money, which he put into his experiments.

On November 6, 1893, shortly before Henry was promoted to chief engineer at the Edison plant, Clara

Clara Jane Bryant and Henry Ford were married on April 11, 1888—the bride's 22nd birthday. In the background is an invitation to their wedding, which was held at the Bryant home.

At left a mustached Henry poses in the dynamo room of the Edison Electric Illuminating Company in Detroit with fellow employees William Bartels *(center)* and George Cato in 1893. That same year Henry's son, Edsel *(above)*, was born. Both Henry and Clara doted on their only child.

gave birth to their only child, a son they named Edsel Bryant Ford. The couple adored Edsel, who was named after Henry's closest childhood friend. Henry loved showing Edsel how to use gadgets and in time set up a workshop so his son could tinker with machines as Henry had as a boy.

As much as Henry delighted in family life, he never lost sight of his dream of building a vehicle that would run under its own power. The more he experimented, the more he became convinced that a gasoline engine—rather than steam or electric — was the best power source. The gasoline engines of the time were noisy and dirty, but Henry knew he could improve them. Clara was even more confident than he was.

On Christmas Eve, 1893, Clara was beginning dinner preparations for a family gathering the next day at their new home at 58 Bagley Avenue in Detroit. But Henry wanted to test a gasoline engine he was working on. He moved the engine from his workshop out back into the kitchen so Clara could help him. While Clara dripped gasoline into the engine's intake, Henry turned the flywheel. After several false starts, the engine roared to life, filling the kitchen with black smoke and gasoline fumes. Edsel, only seven weeks old, slept soundly through the commotion.

For the next few years Henry devoted every spare moment to working on his gas-powered vehicle. Finally, early in the morning of June 4, 1896, he was finished.

Henry was eager to take his "quadricycle" for its first test drive, but there was a problem. The machine was too wide to fit through the doors of the shed. Henry didn't let that stop him. Picking up an ax, he knocked down part of the brick walls, wheeled

This 1953 Norman Rockwell painting was commissioned for Ford Motor Company's 50th anniversary. Henry, with Clara by his side, builds his quadricycle in the shed behind their Bagley Avenue home in 1896. A replica of the shed can be seen at Greenfield Village.

Henry shows off his quadricycle on a Detroit street a few months after he first drove it out of the Bagley Avenue shed *(top)*. According to Henry, "[I]t was considered something of a nuisance, for it made a racket and it scared horses." In the background are blueprints for the quadricycle.

his quadricycle out into the rainy street, started the engine, and drove away. Henry was overjoyed.

For the next several days, Henry drove his quadricycle around Detroit. While it was not the first gasoline-powered car in the city, it was still a novelty. And whenever Henry stopped, enthusiastic crowds swarmed around him and his vehicle. Several people, however, yelled out, "Crazy Henry!" "Yes, crazy," Henry would sometimes reply, tapping the side of his head with a finger, "crazy like a fox." He knew he was one step closer to producing a car for the masses.

Thanks to its location along the Great Lakes, Detroit had developed into an important transportation hub. At the end of the 19th century, the city was a major producer of horse-drawn carriages and was evolving into a mecca for aspiring automobile manufacturers. While some people may have made fun of the 33-year-old Henry's efforts to break into the fledgling automobile industry, no one could dispute that he had established himself as a highly respected mechanic and engineer for the Edison Electric Illuminating Company. His supervisor rewarded his good work by inviting Henry to the company's national convention in New York City. There, at a banquet held on August 11, 1896, he met his hero, 49-year-old Thomas Edison.

Edison had predicted that the "horseless carriage" was the coming innovation. Seated at the banquet table a distance from the great inventor, Henry observed his colleagues surrounding and talking loudly to the partially deaf Edison. The conversation turned to Edison's experiments with the use of storage batteries to run electric vehicles. Henry's boss, thinking it amusing that an employee of an electric company was working on a vehicle that wasn't powered by electricity, told Edison, as he pointed at Henry, "There's a young fellow who's made a gas car." To the man's surprise, Edison summoned Henry to sit next to him and tell him more.

Henry, shown at left above with Thomas Edison years after their first meeting, idolized the great inventor and treasured his friendship.

Henry took out a pencil, drew a sketch on his menu, and proceeded to tell the great man about his design for an automobile powered by a gasoline engine. An enthusiastic Edison banged his fist on the table and told him: "Young man, that's the thing; you have it. Keep at it. Electric cars must keep near to power stations. The storage battery is too heavy. Steam cars won't do either, for they have to have a boiler and fire. Your car is self-contained — carries its own power plant — no fire, no boiler, no smoke and no steam. You have the thing. Keep at it." Edison's support meant everything to Henry. "No man up to then had given me any encouragement," recalled Henry years later.

A few years after meeting Edison, Henry was offered a promotion to general superintendent of the Edison plant. For Henry the choice between taking on new responsibilities and having time to work on designing an automobile for the masses was easy. With Clara's backing, he quit his job on August 15, 1899, and went into the automobile business.

Automobile manufacturing was a new field, but even back then it was extremely competitive. One estimate indicated that between 1900 and 1908, there were 501 companies manufacturing automobiles in the United States. And 60 percent of these companies failed within a few years of their founding. Despite the risks, Henry was anxious to make his mark.

Because of his strong reputation as a mechanic and innovator, Henry was able to attract a number of prominent investors. Between 1899 and 1902 Henry became a senior official in two automobile companies that ultimately failed. In both cases, final decisions were made by the investors. Henry resented this. Unlike his financial backers, Henry was not interested in selling a few high-priced cars to the wealthy. His goal was to produce a high-quality vehicle that the working class could afford.

Henry always saw failure as a sign that he needed to know something more, and he didn't give up until he discovered what that was. Henry was fiercely resolved to remain true to his instincts, maintain his independence, and control his own

Ford Motor Company's first factory was in this rented building on Mack Avenue in Detroit from 1903 to 1904. Peak daily output was 15 cars. Above is Henry's business card from this period.

destiny as a manufacturer, whatever the costs. He realized that one way to advance his goal was to build a race car. Although few people could afford to drive a car, many were keenly interested in how fast one could go. Success in racing cars gained him publicity and new respect and helped win support for building his dream car.

Thanks to the backing of Alexander Malcomson, a risk-taking Scotsman, Ford Motor Company was incorporated on June 16, 1903. Henry's title was vice president, but he really ran the company. A 10-man team built the first car — the Model A — in a room measuring 250 feet by 50 feet on Mack Avenue in Detroit. Henry needed a logo for his car, so he turned to engineer-designer Childe Harold Wills. Using a printing set he got as a teenager, Wills came up with the design still in use today: an oval with the name Ford written inside. In the first year, 1,000 cars were built, each selling for $750. An optional backseat cost $100 more.

On October 10, 1901, Henry *(left)*, accompanied by mechanic Edward S. "Spider" Huff (not visible), drove his 999 race car on a 10-mile course in 13 minutes, 23$^{4}/_{5}$ seconds to beat his rival, Alexander Winton. (Crouching next to Winton is his sales manager, Charles B. Shanks.) Averaging just under 45 miles per hour, Henry's speed was extraordinary for a motorized vehicle at that time.

"I never thought anything of racing, but the public refused to consider the automobile in any light other than as a fast toy. Therefore...we had to race."

Ford Motor Company produced a number of different automobile models before Henry developed the Model T. Shown here are the company's first automobile, the 1903 Model A *(top);* the 1904 Model C *(center);* and the 1906 Model F. In the background is a blueprint for a vehicle that predates the alphabet models.

From the time he was able to get boyhood friends to build a water wheel next to a schoolyard ditch, Henry showed he had a gift for inspiring others to turn his visions into something concrete and to keep working despite seemingly impossible odds. When it came to cars, Henry realized that other men were better at reading blueprints or machining materials. The genius of Henry Ford was his ability to foresee the extraordinary potential of the automobile market and to relentlessly push production to meet demand.

Among the talented people who would play a key role in the success of Henry's new company were James Couzens and logo—and auto—designer Wills. Both were bright, hardworking, and strong-willed. They earned Henry's respect by not hesitating to stand up to him. Wills and Henry had become good friends when they worked together designing race cars. Couzens had been a clerk in Malcomson's coal company. He became indispensable in managing accounts, advertising, sales, marketing, and planning.

When Edsel was 13 years old, Henry gave him a 1906 Model N Ford. Here he uses it to tow friends on their sleds along a snow-covered neighborhood street. As young as age 10, Edsel was taking his mother shopping in his red Model A Runabout.

Core to Henry's philosophy was the importance of staying with a single model of his automobile. Many other manufacturers felt that in order to generate sales it was necessary to bring out a new model every year and make it so unlike previous models that consumers would want to buy the new model. Henry believed firmly that when a model was settled on, "then every improvement on that model should be interchangeable with the old model." This meant a customer could update a car without having to purchase a new one.

For the next several years, Ford Motor Company's engineers worked on new automobile designs — the so-called alphabet models, since each was named for a different letter of the alphabet. Each model brought the Ford team closer to Henry's dream car — a combination of design features and affordability that would make it more of a necessity than a luxury.

On July 6, 1906, Henry Ford was elected president of Ford Motor Company by the company's shareholders. By this time Henry had acquired a majority of the company's stock. Being president and chief stockholder meant that he had the final word on anything to do with Ford Motor Company. His fairness and his mechanical skills were admired by his workers, and his sense of fun and love of practical jokes made him seem approachable. Henry was known to wrestle with his workers, challenge them to footraces across the factory floor, or even hand out an exploding cigar as a gag.

In 1908, after years of experimentation, Henry finally had his dream car. The Model T was born in a small room on the third floor of what was then the Ford factory on Piquette Avenue. Henry and his design team sketched their ideas on a blackboard. Then, using old and new automotive parts, they assembled a model car. In the middle of it all, offering advice and encouragement from his rocking chair, was Henry Ford.

Henry focused all of his energies on the Model T. He was determined to make the final vehicle as strong as but lighter in weight than any other cars at that time. He pushed the Ford team to figure out how they could lessen the weight of steel — the basic building material of the automobile. Henry's team ultimately settled on vanadium steel as a solution to the weight problem. Vanadium is a metallic element that makes steel stronger and more resistant to corrosion, yet it is lighter and less expensive than similar steel alloys.

Weight wasn't the Model T's only distinctive feature. The vehicle was raised

A Model T churns up a dust storm on a dirt road — still the rule rather than the exception in the early 1900s. The extraordinary popularity of the Model T helped to make road improvement a national priority. In the background are blueprints for the Model T's axle and wheels.

"The greatest need today is a light, low-priced car with an up-to-date engine of ample horsepower, and built of the very best material. One that will go anywhere a car of double the horsepower will; that is in every way an automobile and not a toy."

high enough off the ground that it wouldn't get swallowed up and possibly damaged by the ruts of the dirt roads common at that time. The Model T was also the first car in production with its steering on the left side of the vehicle. Before the Model T, the steering was on the right side so drivers could see how close they were to falling into a ditch or rut. But as more streets were paved, Ford designers thought it made more sense to have the steering on the left so the driver could better observe oncoming traffic. Soon after the Model T was in production, other automakers realized that this approach made sense and followed Ford's lead.

Nimbleness and durability—key selling points of the Model T—are reflected in this cartoon. While a Model T scales a mountain peak with ease, its competitor sticks to sites along the main road.

Advertisements announcing that Ford was selling a new 4-cylinder, 20-horsepower, 5-passenger car for $850 created a huge demand for the Model T. It rapidly outsold all other automobiles. During the 1908–1909 season, Ford sold 10,607 Model T's, and the numbers grew significantly for years to come. Anticipating that the company's production facilities would need to be much larger and more specialized to keep up with the demand, Henry purchased approximately 60 acres of land on the northwest edge of Detroit as the site of Ford Motor's new automobile factory. He hired the renowned architect Albert Kahn to build the sprawling Highland Park plant, which opened on New Year's Day, 1910.

It's difficult now to imagine what society was like before the automobile became available to the working class. Most people relied on horse-drawn vehicles, steam locomotives, or riverboats to travel across the country. In urban areas, they rode streetcars or bicycles to get from place to place. As a result, many people seldom traveled more than 10 to 15 miles from their homes. Most Americans were largely isolated from the social and economic life of the nation. Just planning a trip to town was a major undertaking, let alone crossing the state or traveling to the other side of the country. Roads were often just paths in the dirt. There was no need to pave them for horses or horse-drawn vehicles.

The Model T changed all that. Just as Henry predicted, the automobile rapidly went from being a luxury item for the well-to-do to a necessity for the average American. The affordable automobile had an enormous impact on the American consumer. More than anything, it gave car owners independence. Instead of having to go to a train station and follow scheduled train routes, people could hop into their automobiles and travel wherever they wanted to go, whenever they wanted—and at lower cost. City dwellers now could enjoy drives through the countryside, and rural Americans were no longer stuck on the farm.

The popularity of the automobile in American society increased the pressure to improve roads. The rise of the automobile also brought new architecture to the American landscape: service stations, dealerships for both new and used cars, parking lots, motels, shopping centers, and garages for businesses and private residences. The Model T seemed to be virtually everywhere and in its early years was offered mostly in black. Imagine trying to find your car in a parking lot filled with Model T's.

An important part of Henry's business philosophy was providing the best possible service to the customer. Henry insisted on building strong customer relations through reliable service and authorized Ford dealerships. The dealerships were to be clean and fully stocked with Ford parts and have well-equipped repair shops staffed with qualified mechanics. Henry wanted buyers to keep coming back.

As demand for the Model T grew, machines were constantly being developed at Highland Park to do what a worker could do, only faster and more efficiently. The company needed mostly semi-skilled workers who could be trained to do a single task on an assembly line. Before the assembly line, automobiles were built by small teams of highly skilled mechanics—an expensive and time-consuming process.

Henry and his managers were always on the lookout for ways to save manpower, time, and money. To increase the speed and efficiency of production, Henry tried to minimize the physical labor of workers on the assembly line by figuring out how machines could take over more work. The Highland Park plant became a model of industrial efficiency. Its continuously moving assembly line reduced the production time for a Model T from 728 minutes to 93. Yet this business success came at a price. Many workers could not bear the mindless repetition of a single task, such as tightening a bolt or attaching a wheel. This monotony eventually led to an increase in absenteeism. Many workers simply became fed up and quit.

Women assemble magnetos — the part that provides the spark to start an engine — at the Highland Park plant around 1913. Such monotonous work was terrifying to Henry, who admitted, "I could not possibly do the same thing day in and day out."

On January 5, 1914, Ford Motor Company announced a bold solution to this labor problem: the $5 Day. Workers would earn a minimum of $5 per day—nearly double the average wage being made by workers throughout the automotive industry. In addition, the workday would be reduced from nine hours to eight. The public's reaction to this announcement was electric. Henry was hailed as a friend of the common man.

"Everything is highly systematized in our factory and every possible waste motion is eliminated."

Model T bodies are guided down a ramp at the Highland Park plant in 1913. Each is temporarily placed on a chassis. At the freight yard the bodies, wheels, and chassis will be loaded separately to gain space.

After the $5 Day was announced in 1914, a crowd gathered outside the Highland Park plant on Manchester Street. This new wage solved the absentee problem and made Henry's employees highly motivated to work harder, be more productive, and stay with Ford Motor Company.

New workers flooded into the Detroit area to work in Mr. Ford's factory, and those who were already employed there worked harder and were absent less. For the first time, daily production of the Model T reached one thousand in 1914.

Henry made it clear that the new minimum wage, or "prosperity-sharing" plan, was only for individuals who met a certain level of productivity on the job and led what he considered to be appropriate private lives. That meant a Ford employee had to demonstrate that he treated his family with respect, did not drink alcohol, kept a clean and tidy home, saved part of his wages on a regular basis, and had a good moral character. To enforce this policy, Ford Motor created a Sociological Department staffed with individuals who would visit employees' homes and judge their suitability for the new wage. The staff also counseled any employees who needed to reform their personal lives in order to qualify. The largely unskilled immigrant workforce at Ford — mostly from eastern and southern Europe at this time — put up with this invasion into their private lives in exchange for obtaining higher wages and working in a clean, well-ventilated, and safe factory environment.

In 1922 Ford Motor announced another reform. The workweek was reduced from six days to five. This gave the workers more time to rest and spend with their families, and increased management's expectations that its workforce would be more productive while on the job.

Henry was popular with the public, in large part because he looked at

Model T owners found creative uses for their vehicles. A minister converted his into a mobile chapel *(top)*, a farmer substituted spike wheels so he could pull a reaper *(center)*, while another used his to haul hay.

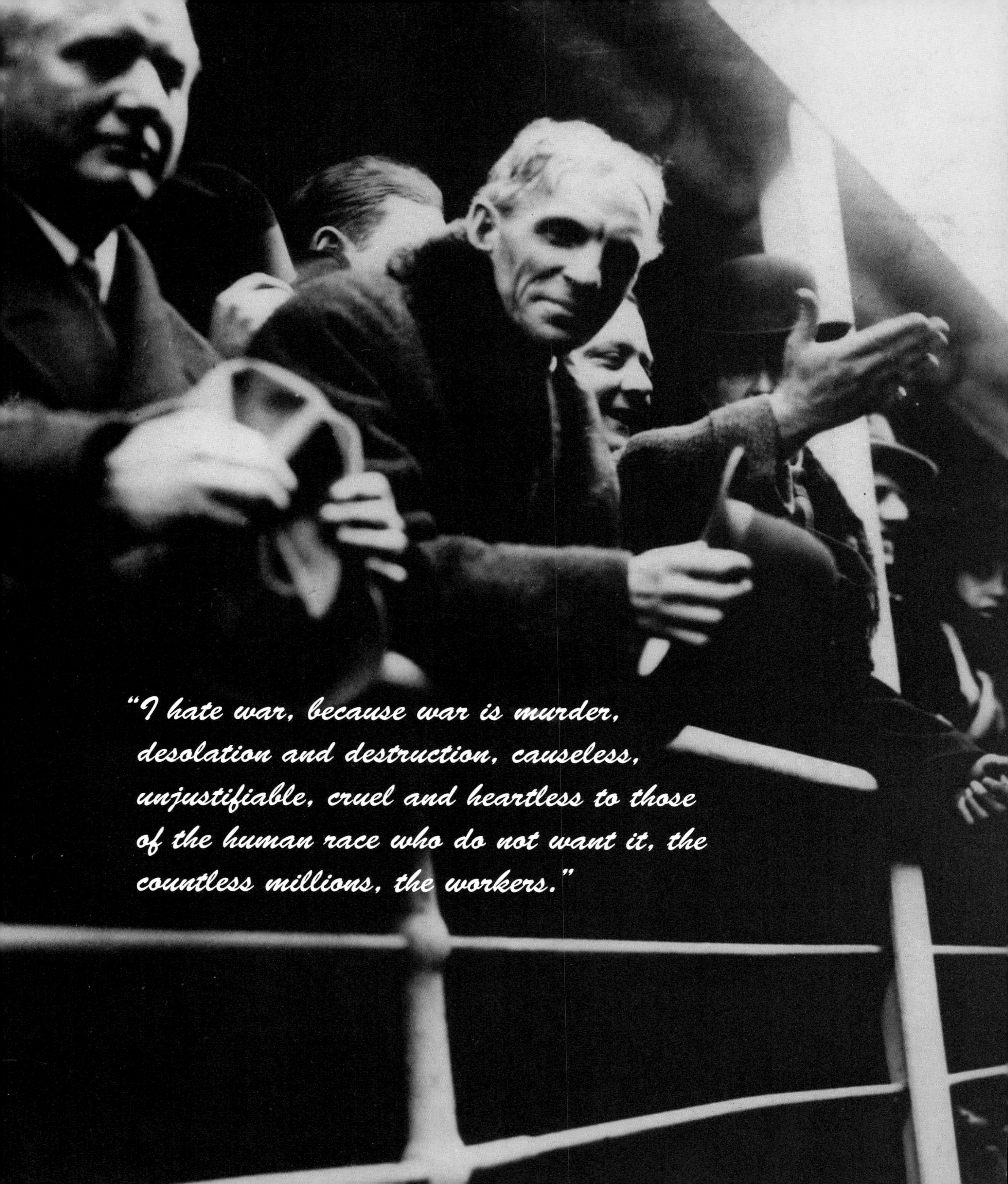

"I hate war, because war is murder, desolation and destruction, causeless, unjustifiable, cruel and heartless to those of the human race who do not want it, the countless millions, the workers."

his employees as partners in the production process. He gave many people work opportunities that they wouldn't have had anywhere else. Henry firmly believed that all people should be given the chance to succeed. For example, at a time of great racial discrimination in the United States, Henry hired many African Americans. Women who were "the sole support of some next of kin" were offered jobs. In addition, people were not rejected because of a physical disability—even if they were blind, deaf, or amputees. Instead, appropriate work was found for them at regular wages. Henry also hired people who had a mental illness or who were former convicts. He felt that the best way to help individuals was to provide them with the chance to help themselves.

With the extraordinary popularity of the Model T, Henry's fame and wealth grew, and his views were sought out by the press. Sometimes this created problems for him. A notable example of this occurred during the First World War. Henry was a pacifist. He believed that his life's mission was to improve, rather than destroy, human life. In 1915 Henry helped finance an effort to end the fighting in Europe. He joined a group of peace activists whose goal was to travel to Europe where they would help create a commission that would try to convince the warring nations to resolve their problems peacefully. Vowing to get the soldiers "out of the trenches by Christmas," Henry chartered the *Oscar II,* or "Peace Ship," which set sail from Hoboken, New Jersey, on December 4, 1915. The mission was a failure, and by 1917 the United States was sending troops to help its allies fight the Germans.

Henry sets sail for Europe with fellow pacifists on board the "Peace Ship." The press was quick to label this well-intentioned effort to end World War I as hopelessly naïve. The mission failed, but Henry claimed he never regretted the effort.

Henry's pacifist views didn't prevent him from authorizing Ford Motor Company to produce trucks, ambulances, cars, and airplane engines for use in the war effort. But he didn't give up on his goal of pursuing peace. Henry supported President Wilson's plan for a League of Nations, an international organization that would promote world peace, and in 1918 he made a run for the U.S. Senate but was defeated.

A few weeks after losing the election, 55-year-old Henry stunned almost everyone when he announced that he was stepping down as president of Ford Motor at the end of the year. Edsel, only 25 years old, would take over as the company's new president in 1919.

Edsel shared his father's fascination with automobiles and from an early age had demonstrated a flair for design. As a high school student, Edsel visited Ford Motor almost daily. He'd toss his schoolbooks onto a desk close to Henry's office and help out with the mail or any other small jobs that needed doing. As soon as Henry spotted Edsel's books, he would light up and join his son. A clearly proud Henry would say, "If that kid can only continue the way he is going, I've got one boy I can be proud of."

Edsel, who was extremely bright and capable, skipped college to work in the family business, where he was widely respected for his hard work and consideration of others. On November 1, 1916, Edsel married Eleanor Lowthian Clay, the niece of a prominent Detroit businessman. In time, they would make Henry and Clara the proud grandparents of Henry II, Benson, Josephine, and William.

In announcing his reason for stepping down as president of Ford Motor Company, Henry said, "I have definite ideas and ideals for the good of all. I intend

Edsel poses with his wife, Eleanor, in front of a Lincoln, a prestigious line of cars Edsel persuaded his father to purchase from the Lincoln Motor Company in 1922. Edsel, who had exceptional skill in automotive design and styling, took great pride in developing the Lincoln into Ford's luxury car.

Edsel's children were given small automobiles to drive around their parents' and grandparents' estates. Shown here (circa 1930) is Benson in a full-size Lincoln, Henry II in an imported MG, and Josephine in a small car custom-built for her.

giving them to the public without having them garbled, distorted and misrepresented." Many of Henry's ideas had a positive impact on society, but some did not.

Around the time that Henry decided to step down as president of Ford Motor, he purchased a weekly newspaper called *The Dearborn Independent*. Ironically, the greatest damage to Henry's reputation was self-inflicted — a result of his

Henry's love of nature evolved into highly publicized camping trips with three of his closest friends: tire manufacturer Harvey Firestone, naturalist John Burroughs, and inventor Thomas Edison. They called themselves the Vagabonds. Here, at the Pecktonville, Maryland, camp on July 24, 1921, Ford, Edison, and Firestone *(far right)* are joined by President Warren Harding *(second from right.)*

stewardship of this newspaper. Under the headline, "The International Jew: The World's Problem," the May 22, 1920, issue of *The Dearborn Independent* launched the first of 91 consecutive articles in a campaign directed by Henry to examine this topic in great detail. The specific source of Henry's anti-Semitism and his need to widely publicize these views is unknown, but this bias against Jews was shared by many people in the United States at the time. Henry had always been distrustful of bankers (some of whom were Jews), and his views appear to have centered on his belief that wealthy and influential people within the Jewish community could, and did, control world events.

The Dearborn Independent was distributed primarily through Ford dealerships nationwide, and dealers were pressured to sell the newspaper aggressively to the public. In 1919 the paper's circulation was 72,000. Its circulation would rise to 650,000 in 1924, and it would grow to 900,000 by 1926. The many articles attacking Jews that were published in *The Dearborn Independent* would be included in a series of book anthologies entitled *The International Jew* that were published in 16 languages.

Many people, including Edsel and Clara, were concerned about Henry's attack against Jews and the damage it was doing to his reputation and that of Ford Motor Company. Many Jewish firms and individuals stopped purchasing Ford vehicles, and Woodrow Wilson as well as some other former U.S. presidents condemned his anti-Semitic articles. But Henry refused to end his campaign.

Ultimately, it took a one-million-dollar libel lawsuit filed by Aaron Sapiro, a Jewish lawyer and farm cooperative leader, to make Henry work out a settlement. In July 1927 Henry issued a lengthy public apology, and by the end of the year, *The Dearborn Independent* had ceased publication at Henry's direction. From that time on, Henry would keep his views on this subject more or less to himself.

Many of Henry's other ideas had a far more positive impact. With the extraordinary success of the Model T and the rapid growth of Ford Motor Company, Henry had the resources and made the time to pursue—among other things—his unique approach to philanthropy.

Henry's personal motto was "Help the Other Fellow," but he didn't believe in simply giving handouts to the less fortunate. Henry declared, "I have no patience with professional charity or with any sort of commercialized humanitarianism." He felt that handouts discourage productivity and self-reliance.

For example, it was important to Henry to make sure that his employees, as well as the broader community, had quality medical care. Of the medical facilities Henry assisted, the largest was the Henry Ford Hospital. Henry directed his staff to examine the most prestigious hospitals in the country and borrow the best ideas from them in building his hospital, which opened its doors to patients in 1915. He recruited highly regarded health professionals to serve in his hospital, and charged low, fixed fees to all patients — regardless of income — so all could receive the best possible care. Henry rightly observed, "There are plenty of hospitals for the rich. There are plenty of hospitals for the poor. There are no hospitals for those who can afford to pay only a moderate amount and yet desire to pay without a feeling that they are recipients of charity.... This hospital is designed to be self-supporting — to give a maximum of service at a minimum of cost and without the slightest colouring of charity."

Physically disabled individuals whom Henry thought could benefit from medical treatment at the hospital were sent there for stays up to a year, with all expenses paid if necessary. He generously gave millions to the hospital over the years, and the facility remains one of the finest medical centers in the country.

Despite the fact that his formal education ended after the sixth grade, Henry had a lifelong interest in and commitment to education. Again, his support of education was based on his own distinctive view that education should impart practical skills: "An educated man is not one whose memory is trained to carry a few dates in history — he is one who can accomplish things. A man who cannot think is not an educated man however many college degrees he may have acquired."

For Henry, formal education supplemented life experience. "A man's real education begins after he has left school. True education is gained through the discipline of life." Here, Henry reviews a young girl's lessons at a school he financed in Saline, Michigan.

Henry's first experiment in the field of education was in 1911, when he invited 10 homeless boys to attend public school while living on one of the farms he owned in Dearborn. Henry paid for the boys' expenses. In return, they were expected to perform simple tasks on the farm. The program's success ultimately led him to begin the Henry Ford Trade School in 1916, next to his Highland Park factory. The school taught skills such as mechanics, drafting, and welding to local boys. Over the years, 8,000 students would graduate from this school, and many would go on to hold important positions in Ford Motor Company. Henry also created the Edison Institute school system, which provided education for thousands of students from kindergarten through high school, without charging any tuition. The buildings and grounds of Henry's museum at Greenfield Village served as its campus. Henry and Clara also donated to dozens of educational institutions in the United States and overseas.

From the time he was old enough to do chores on the family farm, Henry had had a keen interest in improving agriculture. He believed that "[f]arming ought to be more than a rural occupation. It ought to be the business of raising food." It is estimated that in his lifetime Henry purchased more than 3 million acres of farmland, not only in Michigan but also in Georgia, Florida, and other states. The 2.5 million acres of tropical forest he owned in Brazil were a source for the production of rubber for his automobiles. But the approximately 26,000 acres Henry acquired in southeastern Michigan were of particular interest because he personally managed this farmland. During the Depression years of the 1930s, just about anyone out of work and living in the Dearborn area could find work there.

One of the most visionary aspects of Henry's desire to help the farmer was his lifelong commitment to find new industrial uses for farm crops. Henry established a laboratory in Greenfield Village, in Dearborn, to examine the most promising plants. He ultimately concluded that soybeans were the ideal crop. During 1932–33, Henry is said to have spent more than a million dollars on experiments involving 300 varieties of soybeans on more than 8,000 acres of his farmland. He used soybean oil to make paints, soaps, linoleum, and enamels, to name only a few products.

Henry the visionary was decades ahead of others in foreseeing the need to develop a renewable source of energy. He realized early on that a substitute for gasoline needed to be developed, so he directed experiments in alternatives to gasoline that used alcohol derived from agricultural products.

Henry was also determined to preserve history, but in his own way. Henry believed that history, as taught in the schools, put too great an emphasis on war, politics, and wealthy elites and failed to show how everyday people actually lived.

"With One Foot On the Land and One Foot In Industry America Is Safe" . . . . Henry Ford

Henry's firm belief in the link between agriculture and industry *(background poster)* led to generous support for the research not only of famed botanist George Washington Carver (*left*) but also of a crop-based substitute for gasoline.

"All the world is waiting for a substitute for gasoline. When that is gone, there will be no more gasoline, and long before that time, the price of gasoline will have risen to a point where it will be too expensive to burn as a motor fuel."

He became determined to build his own kind of museum to house his vast collection. What would become known as The Henry Ford was dedicated as the Edison Institute of Technology in Dearborn in 1929. Adjoining the museum is Greenfield Village, a 90-plus acre complex of buildings associated not only with Henry's life but also with the lives of other famous Americans (for example, the Wright brothers' bicycle shop and a replica of Edison's Menlo Park laboratory).

Throughout his involvement with these projects, Henry never lost sight of developments at Ford Motor Company. The ten millionth Model T drove out of the factory on June 4, 1924. The high volume of sales made it possible to reduce the price of a car and still allow Ford to make enormous profits. For example, in 1922 the Model T's price fell from $325 to $269. The more the price fell, the more vehicles were sold, and the more profits were made by Ford Motor Company. In 1923–1924, two-thirds of all the automobiles registered in the United States were Model T's.

It can be argued that Henry's single greatest contribution to the success of Ford Motor Company in its early years was his insistence on constantly increasing production of the simple, reliable, and affordable Model T. In 1915 he began purchasing several thousand acres of land southwest of Dearborn along the River Rouge, where he built a massive industrial complex. The sprawling River Rouge complex included shipping and railroad facilities, furnaces for steelmaking, a sawmill, a concrete plant, a power plant, a body plant, and an assembly plant. The money the company saved in production costs was passed on to the consumer. Other Ford production and assembly plants were built across the United States and around the world to satisfy the growing demand. By 1928 Ford Motor had shifted most of its production to the River Rouge facility.

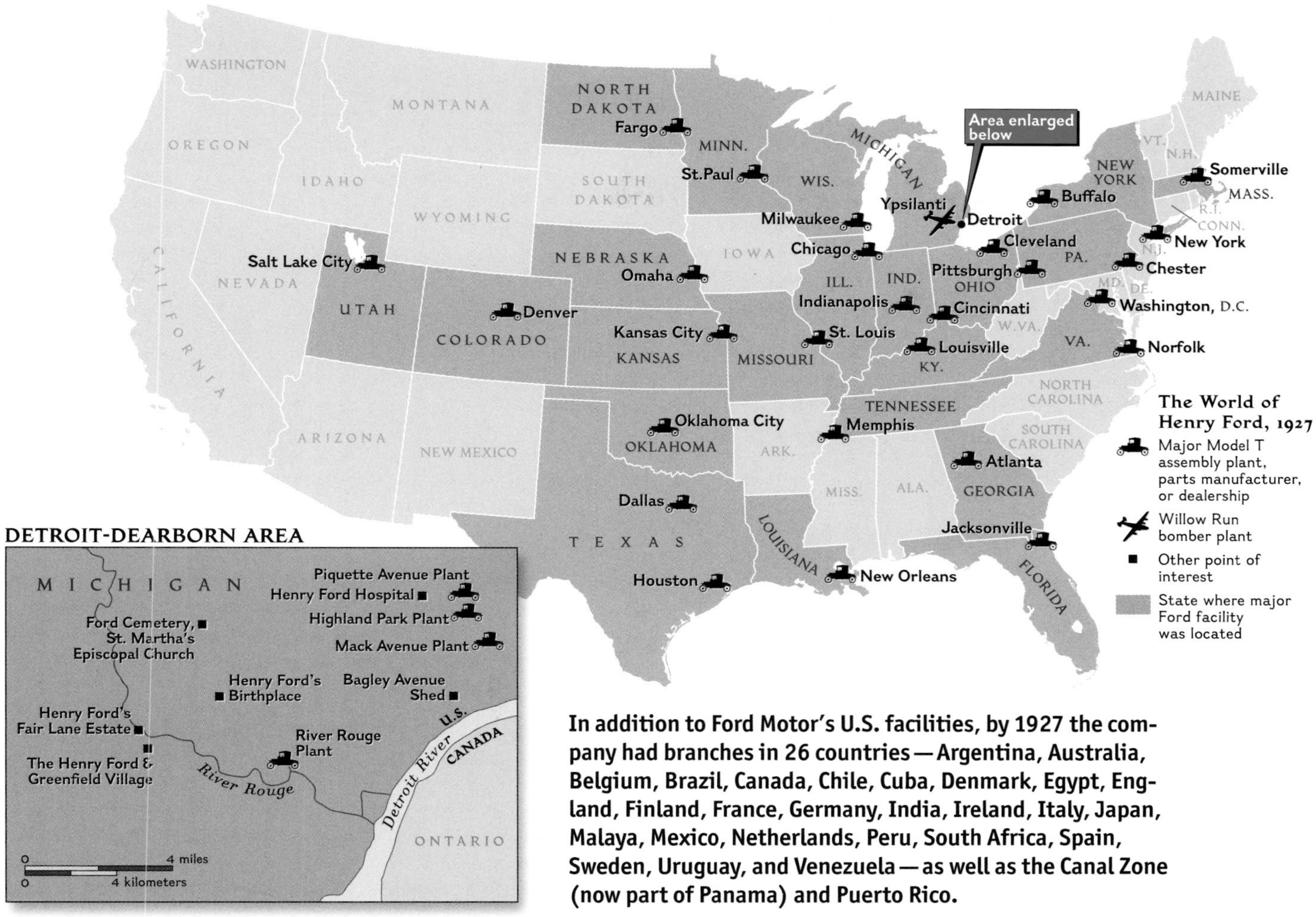

The World of Henry Ford, 1927

Major Model T assembly plant, parts manufacturer, or dealership

Willow Run bomber plant

Other point of interest

State where major Ford facility was located

DETROIT-DEARBORN AREA

In addition to Ford Motor's U.S. facilities, by 1927 the company had branches in 26 countries—Argentina, Australia, Belgium, Brazil, Canada, Chile, Cuba, Denmark, Egypt, England, Finland, France, Germany, India, Ireland, Italy, Japan, Malaya, Mexico, Netherlands, Peru, South Africa, Spain, Sweden, Uruguay, and Venezuela—as well as the Canal Zone (now part of Panama) and Puerto Rico.

As Henry oversaw the explosive growth of the River Rouge facility, he became increasingly isolated from changes that were going on in the automobile industry. Consumer interest was moving away from simple vehicles like the Model T to higher-performing, more stylish, and more comfortable vehicles. Ford's major competitor, General Motors (GM), was coming up with creative ways to make these models affordable, such as permitting customers to purchase vehicles on an installment plan and allowing them to trade in a used car as a down payment for a new car. GM also offered so-called model-year changes, which offered new features annually in a particular model. Henry clung to the unrealistic belief that the Model T was the only automobile people would ever need or want.

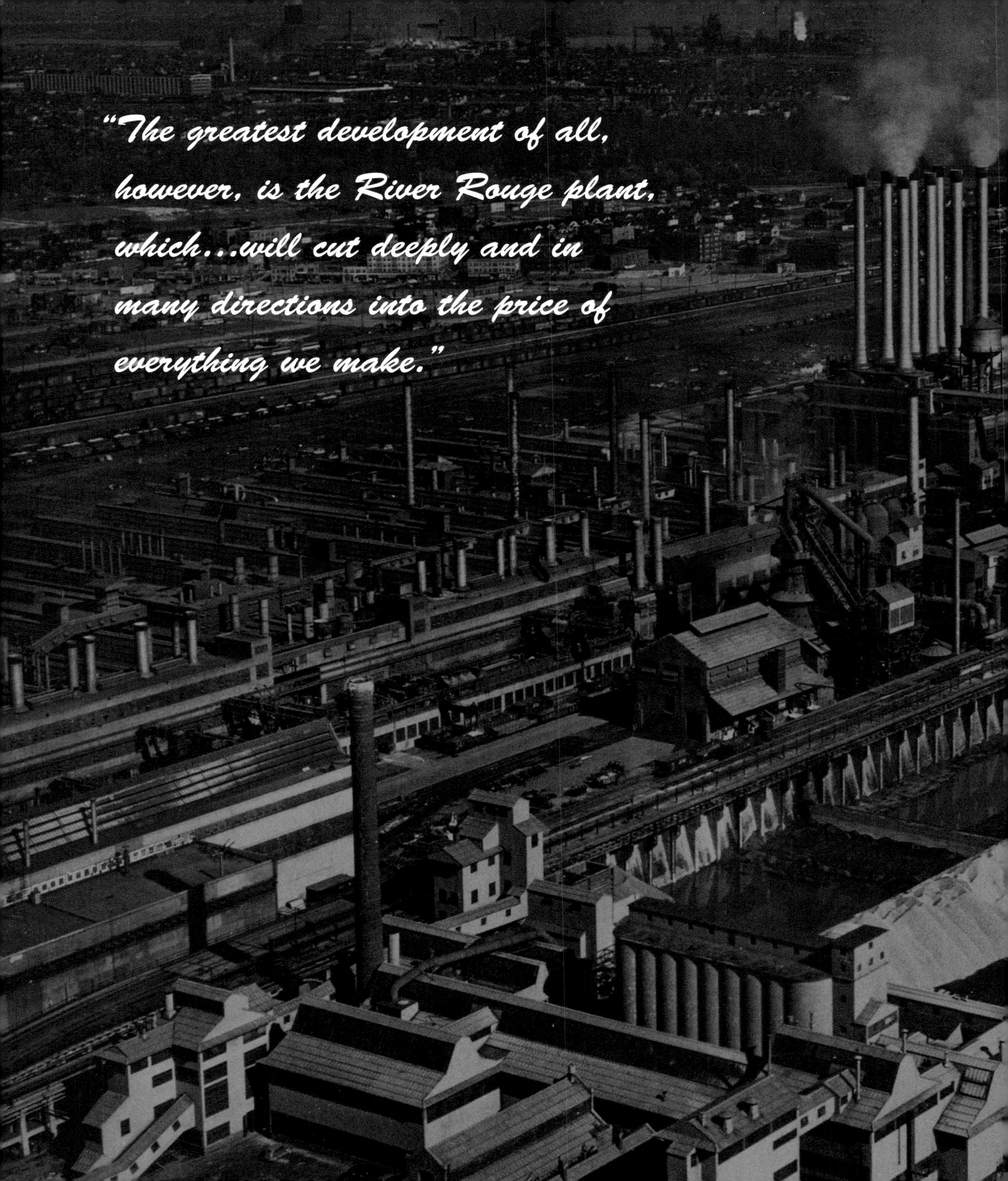
“The greatest development of all, however, is the River Rouge plant, which...will cut deeply and in many directions into the price of everything we make.”

This aerial view (circa 1928) shows only a portion of the sprawling River Rouge complex. To support the Rouge facility, Henry acquired his own railroad, ships, mines, and timberlands. By controlling all aspects of production — including shipping and railroad facilities, a sawmill, a concrete plant, a body plant, and an assembly plant — Ford Motor could enjoy huge cost savings and pass them on to the consumer.

Henry believed the Model T was perfect in its basic form. While he supported mechanical improvements, he saw no need for any changes in the car's design. As early as 1912 Ford engineers had surprised him with an updated version of the Model T that they thought would be more competitive in the market. An enraged Henry walked around the car several times and then tore off the doors, smashed the windshield, and ripped the top. The message was clear: the Model T was a winning formula that was not to be changed.

But competition from other automakers eager to satisfy consumer demand for change finally convinced Henry to move beyond the Model T. On May 26, 1927, Henry and Edsel drove the 15 millionth Model T off the assembly line at Highland Park. Then the company announced its successor: the Model A. It represented such a notable change that Ford went back to the beginning of the alphabet to name it. Production of the new car would require a massive

The powerful Model A created a sensation when it was unveiled to the public. It could accelerate up to 65 miles per hour and was more comfortable than the Model T. Here, Model A Victoria Coupes are being produced on the River Rouge assembly line in 1931.

industrial changeover. Ford Motor shut down production for five months to retool the River Rouge facility and the company's other assembly plants. By the time the new Model A began rolling off assembly lines in November 1927, the company had spent approximately $250 million.

Initially, the Model A was popular with consumers and sold well, but Ford Motor no longer claimed such a large share of the automobile market as it had in the early days of the Model T. Then, in 1929, the nation's economy began to collapse in what became known as the Great Depression. It hit Ford Motor Company and other American businesses hard. By 1931 sales of the Model A were down sharply. As profits declined, Ford was forced to lay off workers, contributing to the high unemployment rate in Detroit and throughout the country.

Henry was strongly opposed to President Franklin Roosevelt's New Deal programs for offering economic relief from the Depression. Of particular concern were plans aimed at improving working conditions for labor in areas such as wages, work hours, and asserting the right of workers to organize and bargain collectively for more favorable working conditions without fearing retaliation from employers. Henry felt that the key to success was individual initiative and self-reliance. He saw government efforts to regulate the country's social and economic life as disastrous for the nation. He distrusted labor unions as much as he distrusted banks and other financial interests. Henry didn't want the government, unions, or anyone else telling him how he should run his company.

The 1930s saw growing tension between Ford Motor Company's management and its labor force. Henry became convinced that people were out to challenge his authority. It rapidly became apparent that Henry, in turning over the title of company president to his son, had not handed over any meaningful authority. While Edsel played a key role in the company's management, Henry continued to make all the major decisions. He would consistently undermine Edsel's authority by overruling his orders and encouraging other Ford managers to take positions that went against Edsel's directives. The senior officials at Ford Motor always knew that it was in their best interest to support Henry whenever there was a difference of opinion between father and son.

Despite the challenges to his authority, Edsel always tried to remain obedient and loyal to his father. Many believe that Henry's treatment of Edsel was a form of "tough love" designed to make his son more combative and to harden him to the challenging business world. He didn't believe Edsel was sufficiently tough-minded to manage the day-to-day activities at Ford Motor, yet Henry no longer had the energy to oversee all aspects of the work being done by the company. So, during the difficult economic climate of the 1930s, Henry turned increasingly to a man named Harry Bennett.

Hired by Henry during the First World War, Harry Bennett was an unruly street brawler who charmed Henry with his independence, toughness, and irreverent humor. With Henry's support, Bennett rose rapidly within the company. Given a free hand to deal with the company's labor problems—and just about everything else—Bennett used fear and threats to exercise his authority. He did away with the company's Sociological Department and replaced it with a Service Department comprised largely of gangsters and ex-convicts. He used the Service Department to spy on workers and executives alike.

Henry suffered the first of several strokes in 1937. As his physical and mental health declined, he relied more than ever on Harry Bennett to run the company.

As both employment and production continued to decline at Ford Motor during the Depression, the quality of life of the company's remaining workers worsened sharply under the new regime. Foremen drove workers hard on the assembly line, and Bennett's men beat up or fired workers for even minor offenses, real or imaginary. Losing workers was not a concern. Everyone knew that for every worker fired there were plenty of others standing in line to take their places.

Edsel and Henry examine the V-8 engine in a 1935 Fordor Sedan Deluxe. The powerful new engine was a big hit with the public.

The harsher the environment at Ford Motor became, the more the workers were drawn to labor unions — which were forbidden from organizing at Ford — as a way of protecting themselves against the company's management practices. This in turn made management stand firm in its opposition to unions. Conflict was inevitable. A bloody confrontation came on May 26, 1937, when Bennett's security thugs beat up some union organizers from the United Auto Workers (UAW) who were handing out pro-union leaflets in a public area outside the River Rouge plant.

The attack created a national furor, and Henry's reputation as a compassionate champion of the average worker was severely damaged. Ford Motor's opposition to unions continued over the next several years, even as automakers General Motors and Chrysler made peace with the unions and allowed the UAW to organize within their companies. Despite the loss of several lawsuits and of favorable public opinion, Henry adamantly continued to fight the unions.

The crisis came to a head on April 1, 1941. The UAW, in an effort to pressure Ford management to allow its workers to unionize, called on Ford workers to go out on strike to shut down the River Rouge facility. Edsel urged Henry to end the strike by settling with the union so that production could continue, but Henry stubbornly vowed to fight the UAW to the bitter end. Clara, appalled at the violence and the damage to the company it was causing, told her husband she would leave him if he didn't settle the labor dispute. Henry gave in.

The Ford workforce voted overwhelmingly to be represented by the UAW. On June 20, 1941, Ford Motor Company signed a historic agreement with the United Auto Workers that at the time was the most generous in the history of industrial relations. Ford workers were given even more than what the union demanded, such as providing back pay to wrongfully discharged workers and agreeing to match the highest wage rates in the industry. Once Henry accepted an idea, he always wanted it done right.

The settlement came less than six months before Japan attacked the United States at Pearl Harbor, Hawai'i, and its ally Germany declared war on the United States in December 1941. Not surprisingly, pacifist Henry had opposed American involvement in World War II, accusing all sides of being motivated by greed. But all that changed with the actions of Japan and Germany. Ford Motor became a leading producer of tanks, cargo trucks, gliders, and aircraft engines

The dispute between Ford Motor and the United Auto Workers (UAW) erupted into violence on May 26, 1937, outside the main entrance to the Rouge plant *(background photo)*. UAW organizer Richard Frankensteen *(right)* was among those beaten by Ford security men in what became known as the Battle of the Overpass. The billboard was one of several erected by the UAW in 1938 close to the Rouge property.

B-24 bombers await final assembly at Willow Run in February 1943. Each bomber contained 550,000 parts (not including 700,000 rivets), could fly 3,000 miles without refueling, and could hold as much as 4 tons of bombs. The timely delivery of these complex aircraft was a testament to the success of Henry's assembly-line techniques.

Henry's grandson Henry Ford II *(far left)* meets with Harry Bennett in Bennett's office in 1944. The two men detested each other and fought for control of Ford Motor during Henry's declining years. Many in the company hoped that young Henry would prevail and put an end to years of mismanagement and in-fighting.

for the country and its allies, helping to earn Detroit the nickname "arsenal of democracy." The company invested approximately $50 million in constructing a massive aircraft production facility along a stream called Willow Run, some 20 miles west of Dearborn. By using assembly-line production techniques, the company produced more than 8,600 B-24 Liberator bombers by war's end.

Years of management disagreements with his father, coupled with the bitter labor dispute, left Edsel physically and emotionally exhausted. His health had so deteriorated by early 1943 that he wanted to resign as president of Ford Motor. Henry ignored the idea, refusing to take his son's health issues seriously. A few months later, on May 26, Edsel died of stomach cancer.

A devastated Henry blamed himself for his son's death. Clara, who had always resented the way Henry treated Edsel after their son took over the company, was now more bitter than ever. The shattered couple could not bring themselves to discuss Edsel. Indeed, for a while after their son's funeral, they barely spoke to each other at all. Finally, weeks after Edsel's death, Clara realized that she needed to rescue her husband from his depression. One morning, she handed him a basket and garden shears and said, "Henry, the peonies are in bloom. We need a big jar of them for the front hall. Let's go and see what we can find." They worked quietly side by side in their magnificent garden at Fair Lane. By the time they were done gathering flowers, they had found their way back together again.

On June 1, 1943, Henry was elected president of Ford Motor Company at a special meeting of the board of directors. But it soon became clear that he was no longer mentally capable of serving in this position. When Henry made Harry Bennett acting head of the company, Edsel's widow, Eleanor—with Clara's support—argued that her eldest son, 25-year-old Henry Ford II, should become president. Henry wouldn't hear of it and continued to support Bennett. Nevertheless, Henry's grandson was released from service in the U.S. Navy to help in the company's management. World War II was still going on, but the contribution of Ford Motor Company to the war effort made Henry Ford II more valuable to the country working at home than fighting overseas.

Henry and Clara carve their initials into a tree on the lawn of their Fair Lane estate. Behind them is Clara's prize peony garden. About his partner of nearly 60 years, Henry said, "If I were to die and come back to another life, I would want the same wife."

The young Ford displayed toughness and determination and worked hard to learn the business, assembling a team of capable and trusted advisers. Then, in early 1945 Henry suffered another stroke, which left him in a confused state. Both Clara and Eleanor urged Henry to step aside and allow Henry II to formally take control of the company. When Henry still refused, the Ford women threatened to sell their company stock. Unable to bear the thought of such a significant amount of company stock passing out of the family's hands, Henry announced his resignation on September 21, 1945. Henry Ford II was formally named president of Ford Motor Company, and Harry Bennett was fired. In the next several years, Henry Ford II would prove his worth by restoring the company to a profitable peacetime enterprise and innovative leader in the automobile industry.

Tens of thousands paid their respects at Henry's funeral. Flags all over Detroit flew at half-mast, and every Ford Motor plant and showroom around the world was closed.

Henry lived out the rest of his days at his Fair Lane estate, where Clara lovingly cared for him. Confused by and mistrustful of the modern world he had done so much to create, Henry yearned for an earlier era that, ironically, his Model T had done so much to destroy. Henry Ford died of a cerebral hemorrhage on April 7, 1947, at the age of 83. Although he died just a few miles from where he was born, Henry had traveled far during his life's journey, and he took the rest of the world along for the ride.

AFTERWORD

A complex individual, Henry Ford was an idealist in his early years. He was convinced that his ideas could not only bring about business success but also benefit all of society. His enormous popularity with "the common man" was not surprising. Henry improved the life of the working man by paying high wages, providing a safe and clean work environment, and employing minorities and disabled individuals at a time when many other organizations were unwilling to do so. As a reformer, he actively sought to improve the quality of life of his employees and make them better citizens through his intrusive, but well-intentioned, Sociological Department.

A committed pacifist, Henry saw war as senseless waste. He was interested in education, providing for the less fortunate, finding industrial uses for agriculture, and preserving traditional American culture, which he did by establishing his industrial museum and Greenfield Village (now part of The Henry Ford) in Dearborn, Michigan. One of the world's wealthiest men, Henry was largely indifferent to money and found creative ways—including his hospitals, farms, and schools— to give generously to others. He thought individuals should be judged by their actions and abilities and not their social standing. Henry's fundamental belief was that technology would bring the world closer together and improve everyone's quality of life.

A pensive Henry sits in a field at Mount Clemens, Michigan, on a summer day in 1919.

Henry had admirers from many walks of life. In the photograph below, Henry autographs baseballs at a trade school exhibit at the Ford Exposition of Progress in 1934. In the background is a letter to Henry dated May 27, 1946, from deaf-blind activist Helen Keller thanking Henry for his support for people with disabilities.

The photograph above shows bank robbers Clyde Barrow and Bonnie Parker in front of a 1932 Ford V-8. In a fan letter allegedly written by Barrow to Henry on April 10, 1934, the fugitive wrote, "For sustained speed and freedom from trouble the Ford has got ever other car skinned and even if my business hasn't been strictly legal it don't hurt anything to tell you what a fine car you got in the V8." Later that year Bonnie and Clyde were killed by law enforcement officers while driving a stolen Ford V-8.

Yet Henry also launched one of the bitterest campaigns against Jews in American history, used labor spies and winked at violence against suspected union organizers at Ford Motor Company late in his life, and undermined his son's position in the family business — tragically destroying one of the most important relationships in his life.

A 1923 poster showing the Highland Park plant

Like many powerful and famous people, Henry Ford had his critics and his admirers. Yet one fact about Henry Ford is indisputable: He did more than any other single individual to put the world on wheels. Late in his life, he summed up his extraordinary achievement this way: "The Ford car [the Model T] blazed the way for the motor industry and started the movement for good roads. It broke down the barriers of time and distance and helped to place education within the reach of all. It gave people more leisure. It helped everyone to do more and better work in less time and enjoy doing it. It did a great deal, I am sure, to promote the growth and progress of the country."

And so it did.

CHRONOLOGY

1863 Henry Ford is born on July 30 in his parents' farmhouse in a rural area that is now part of Dearborn, Michigan.

1879 Henry leaves home to work in machine shops in Detroit.

1888 Henry marries Clara Jane Bryant on April 11.

1893 Henry and Clara's only child, Edsel Bryant Ford, is born on November 6.

1896 Henry completes creating his gasoline fueled "quadricycle" on June 4 in the shed behind his Bagley Avenue home in Detroit.

1896 Henry meets his hero, inventor Thomas Edison, in New York City on August 11.

1899 On August 5, the Detroit Automobile Company is formed.

1901 The Henry Ford Company is organized with Henry as engineer. In 1902 Henry resigns in a dispute with bankers, and the company becomes the Cadillac Motor Car Company.

1903 Ford Motor Company is incorporated on June 16 with Henry as vice president. The first Model A is offered for sale in Detroit.

1906 Shareholders elect Henry president of Ford Motor Company on July 6.

1908 Ford Motor begins manufacturing its famous Model T.

1910 Ford Motor begins operations at the Highland Park factory.

1913 The world's first moving automobile assembly line is introduced at Highland Park.

1914 Henry announces his plans to share company profits with workers, paying them $5.00 for an 8-hour workday.

1915 Henry's "Peace Ship," the *Oscar II,* sets sail for Norway on a mission to end World War I.

1916 Edsel Ford and Eleanor Clay are married in Detroit on November 1.

1917 Construction of the River Rouge facility begins.

1918 Henry loses his bid for the U.S. Senate.

1919 Son Edsel becomes president of Ford Motor Company.

1927 Ford Motor's assembly line is moved from Highland Park to the River Rouge facility. Production of the Model T ends, and the new Model A is introduced.

1929 Henry dedicates his Edison Institute of Technology and Greenfield Village with "Light's Golden Jubilee," a celebration of 50 years of the electric light.

1937 The Battle of the Overpass occurs between Ford Motor's security staff and United Auto Workers (UAW) union organizers on May 26.

1941 Ford Motor Company signs a historic labor contract with the UAW on June 20.

1943 Edsel dies in his home on May 26. On June 1, Henry becomes president of Ford Motor.

1945 Henry resigns as president of Ford Motor; grandson Henry Ford II becomes president on September 21.

1947 Henry Ford, age 83, dies of a massive cerebral hemorrhage at his Fair Lane estate on April 7.

1950 Clara Ford, age 84, dies of heart failure at Henry Ford Hospital in Detroit on September 29.

1987 Henry Ford II, age 70, dies of pneumonia at Henry Ford Hospital on September 29—exactly 37 years after his grandmother died there.

QUOTE SOURCES

The references noted here are abbreviations for sources fully cited on page 63. Page 5: "I will build a motor car..." Brinkley, p. 113; page 8: "Don't let Henry..." Nevins and Hill, *Ford: The Times, the Man, the Company,* p. 48; "Every clock..." Olson, p. 20; "[t]he house was like a watch..." Ibid., p. 22; page 9: "There was too much hard hand labor..." Ford and Crowther, *My Life and Work,* p. 22; page 11: "was simply a portable engine..." Ibid., p. 22; "but this one had a chain..." Ibid., pp. 22–23; "making a machine..." Ibid, p. 23; pages 12–13: "[t]here is an immense amount..." Ibid., pp. 23–24; page 13: "a first-class workshop" Ibid., p. 29; page 16: "Crazy Henry!...like a fox." Collier and Horowitz, p. 11; "It was considered something of a nuisance..." Ford and Crowther, *My Life and Work,* p. 33; page 17: "There's a young fellow..." Nevins and Hill, *Ford: The Times, the Man, the Company,* p. 167; pages 17–18: "Young man, that's the thing..." Ford and Crowther, *Edison As I Know Him,* p. 5; page 18: "No man up to then..." Ibid., page 5; page 21: "I never thought anything..." Ford and Crowther, *My Life and Work,* p. 36; page 23: "then every improvement..." Ibid., p. 57; page 25: "The greatest need today..." Brinkley, p.100; page 29: "I could not possibly..." Ford and Crowther, *My Life and Work,* p. 103; page 30: "Everything is highly systematized..." Watts, p. 140; page 32: "prosperity sharing," Ford and Crowther, *My Life and Work,* p. 128; page 34: "I hate war..." Ford, p. 7; page 35: "the sole support..." Ford and Crowther, *My Life and Work,* p. 127; "out of the trenches by Christmas" Kraft, p. 68; page 36: "If that kid can only continue..." Nevins and Hill, *Ford: The Times, the Man, the Company,* p. 374; pages 36–37: "I have definite ideas..." Brinkley, p. 238; page 39: "Help the Other Fellow" Lewis, p. 119; "I have no patience..." Ford and Crowther, *My Life and Work,* p. 206; page 40: "There are plenty of hospitals..." Ibid., p. 215; "An educated man..." Ibid., p. 247; page 41: "A man's real education...." Ibid., p. 248; page 42: "[f]arming ought to be more..." Ibid., p. 204; page 43: "All the world is waiting..." Brinkley, p. 219; page 46: "The greatest development..." Ford and Crowther, *My Life and Work,* p. 151; page 55: "Henry, the peonies are in bloom..." Lewis, p. 407; page 56: "If I were to die..." Ibid., p. 479; page 59: "Life, as I see it,..." Ford and Crowther, *My Life and Work,* p. 43; page 60: "For sustained speed..." Lewis, p. 207; page 61: "The Ford car..." Brinkley, pp. 522–523; back cover: "must be..." Brinkley, p. 100.

RESOURCES

BOOKS

The following is a small sampling of the many books written about Henry Ford and the early years of Ford Motor Company:

A History of The Henry Ford: Telling America's Story. Dearborn, MI: The Henry Ford, *2009.*

Bak, Richard. *Henry and Edsel: The Creation of the Ford Empire.* Hoboken, NJ: John Wiley & Sons, Inc., 2003.

Baldwin, Neil. *Henry Ford and the Jews: The Mass Production of Hate.* NY: PublicAffairs, 2001.

Brauer, Norman. *There to Breathe the Beauty: The Camping Trips of Henry Ford, Thomas Edison, Harvey Firestone and John Burroughs.* Dalton, PA: Norman Brauer Publications, 1995.

Brinkley, Douglas. *Wheels for the World: Henry Ford, his Company, and a Century of Progress, 1903–2003.* NY: Viking, 2003.

Bryan, Ford R. *Beyond the Model T: The Other Ventures of Henry Ford.* Detroit, MI: Wayne State University Press, 1997.

________. *Clara: Mrs. Henry Ford.* Dearborn, MI: Ford Books, 2001.

________. *Friends, Families & Forays: Scenes from the Life and Times of Henry Ford.* Dearborn, MI: Ford Books, 2002.

________. *Henry's Lieutenants.* Detroit, MI: Wayne State University Press, 1993.

Cabadas, Joseph P. *River Rouge: Ford's Industrial Colossus.* St. Paul, MN: Motorbooks International, 2004.

Casey, Robert. *The Model T: A Centennial History.* Baltimore, MD: The Johns Hopkins University Press, 2008.

Collier, Peter and David Horowitz. *The Fords: An American Epic.* NY: Summit Books, 1987.

Ford, Henry. "Comments—Peace vs. War." Reprinted from *Detroit Free Press,* August 22, 1915.

Ford, Henry with Samuel Crowther. *My Life and Work.* Garden City, N.Y.: Doubleday, 1922.

________. *Today and Tomorrow.* Garden City, N.Y.: Doubleday, Page and Company, 1926.

________. *Edison as I Know Him.* NY: Cosmopolitan Book Corporation, 1930.

Head, Jeanine and William S. Pretzer. *Henry Ford: A Pictorial Biography.* Dearborn, MI: Henry Ford Museum & Greenfield Village, 1998.

Kraft, Barbara S. *The Peace Ship: Henry Ford's Pacifist Adventure in the First World War.* NY: Macmillan Publishing Co., Inc., 1978.

Lacey, Robert. *Ford, the Men and the Machine.* Boston, MA: Little, Brown and Company, 1986.

Lewis, David L. *The Public Image of Henry Ford: An American Folk Hero and His Company.* Detroit, MI: Wayne State University Press, 1976.

Nevins, Allan and Frank Ernest Hill. *Ford: The Times, the Man, the Company.* NY: Charles Scribner's Sons, 1954.

________. *Ford: Expansion and Challenge, 1915–1933.* NY: Charles Scribner's Sons, 1957.

________. *Ford: Decline and Rebirth, 1933–1962.* NY: Charles Scribner's Sons, 1962.

Olson, Sidney. *Young Henry Ford: A Picture History of the First Forty Years.* Detroit, MI: Wayne State University Press, 1963.

Watts, Steven. *The People's Tycoon: Henry Ford and the American Century.* NY: Alfred A. Knopf, 2005.

White, E.B. *Farewell to Model T; From Sea to Shining Sea.* NY: The Little Bookroom, 2003.

VIDEO

Henry Ford: Tin Lizzy Tycoon, A&E Television Networks, 1994.

RECOMMENDED WEB SITES

The Henry Ford Estate (Fair Lane)
National Historic Landmark
4901 Evergreen Road
Dearborn, MI 48128
(313) 593-5590
www.henryfordestate.org

The Henry Ford Greenfield Village
20900 Oakwood Boulevard
Dearborn, MI 48124
(313) 982-6100
www.thehenryford.org

The Edsel & Eleanor Ford House
1100 Lake Shore Road
Grosse Pointe Shores, MI 48236
(313) 884-4222
www.fordhouse.org

Ford Motor Company
Dearborn, MI 48126
www.ford.com

Edison and Ford Winter Estates
2350 McGregor Boulevard
Fort Myers, FL 33901
(239) 334-7419
www.efwefla.org

INDEX

The National Geographic Society is one of the world's largest nonprofit scientific and educational organizations. Founded in 1888 to "increase and diffuse geographic knowledge," the Society works to inspire people to care about the planet. It reaches more than 325 million people worldwide each month through its official journal, *National Geographic*, and other magazines; National Geographic Channel; television documentaries; music; radio; films; books; DVDs; maps; exhibitions; school publishing programs; interactive media; and merchandise. National Geographic has funded more than 9,000 scientific research, conservation, and exploration projects and supports an education program combating geographic illiteracy. For more information, visit nationalgeographic.com.

For more information, please call 1-800-NGS LINE (647-5463) or write to the following address:

National Geographic Society
1145 17th Street N.W.
Washington, D.C. 20036-4688 U.S.A.

Visit us online at www.nationalgeographic.com/books

For librarians and teachers: www.ngchildrensbooks.org

More for kids from National Geographic: kids.nationalgeographic.com